AROUND the WICKET GATE

AROUND the WICKET GATE

C. H. SPURGEON

Whitaker House

AROUND THE WICKET GATE

ISBN: 0-88368-312-1
Printed in the United States of America
Copyright © 1995 by Whitaker House
Images © 1995 PhotoDisc, Inc.

Whitaker House
580 Pittsburgh Street
Springdale, PA 15144

1 2 3 4 5 6 7 8 9 10 / 04 03 02 01 00 99 98 97 96 95

Contents

Thou art not far from the kingdom of God.
—Mark 12:34

Preface

Millions of people are in outlying regions, far from God and peace. For these we pray, and to these we give warning. However, just now we have to deal with a smaller company who are not far from the kingdom, but have come right up to the wicket gate which stands at the entrance to the way of life. One would think that they would hasten to enter. A free and open invitation is placed over the entrance, the porter waits to welcome them, and there is but this one way to eternal life. He that is most burdened seems the most likely to pass in and begin the heavenward journey, but what ails the other men?

This is what I want to find out. Poor fellows! They have come a long way already to get where they are. The King's highway, which they seek, is right before them. Why do they not take to the Pilgrim Road at once?

Alas! They have a great many reasons. Foolish as those reasons are, it needs a very wise man to answer them all. I cannot pretend to do so. Only the Lord Himself can remove the folly which is bound up in their hearts and lead them to take the great decisive step. Yet the Lord works by means. I have prepared this little book in the earnest hope that He may work by it to the blessed end of leading seekers to an immediate, simple trust in the Lord Jesus.

He who does not take the step of faith and so enter upon the road to heaven will perish. It will be an awful thing to die just outside the gate of life. Almost saved, but altogether lost! This is the most terrible of positions. A man just outside Noah's ark would have been drowned. A manslayer close to the wall of the city of refuge, but yet outside of it, would be slain. The man who is within a yard of Christ, and yet has not trusted Him, will be just as surely lost.

Therefore, am I in terrible earnest to get my hesitating friends over the threshold. "Come in! Come in!" is my pressing entreaty. *"Wherefore standest thou without?"* (Genesis 24:31) is my solemn question. May the Holy Spirit render my pleadings effective with many who will glance at these pages! May He cause His own Almighty power to create faith in the soul at once!

My reader, if God blesses this book to you, do the writer this favor—either lend your own copy to one who is lingering at the gate, or buy another and give it away. My great desire is that this little volume should be of service to many thousands of souls.

To God this book is dedicated, for without His grace nothing will come of anything that is written.

C. H. Spurgeon

Chapter 1

Awakenings

Great numbers of persons have no concern about eternal things. They care more about their cats and dogs than about their souls. It is a great mercy to be forced to think about ourselves, and how we stand in relationship to God and the eternal world. This is often a sign that salvation is coming to us. By nature we do not like the anxiety which spiritual concern causes us, and we try, like sluggards, to sleep again. This is great foolishness. For it is at our peril that we trifle when death is so near and judgment is so sure.

If the Lord has chosen us for eternal life, He will not let us return to our slumber. If we are sensible, we will pray that our anxiety about our souls may never come to an end until we are really and truly saved. Let us say from our hearts:

"He that suffered in my stead,
Shall my Physician be
I will not be comforted
Till Jesus comfort me."

It would be an awful thing to go dreaming down to hell, and there to lift up our eyes with a great gulf fixed between us and heaven. It will be equally terrible to be aroused to escape from the wrath to come, and then to shake off the warning influence and go back to our insensibility. I notice that those who overcome their convictions and continue in their sins are not so easily moved the next time. Every awakening which is thrown away leaves the soul more drowsy than before and less likely to be again stirred to holy feeling. Therefore, our hearts should be greatly troubled at the thought of getting rid of its distress in any other than the right way.

A person who had the gout was cured of it by a quack medicine, which drove the disease within, and the patient died. To be cured of distress of mind by a false hope would be a terrible business. The remedy would be worse than the disease. Better far that our tenderness of conscience should cause us long years of anguish, than that we should lose it and perish in the hardness of our hearts.

Yet awakening is not a thing to rest in, or to desire to have lengthened out month after month. If I start in a fright and find my house on fire, I do not sit down at the edge of the bed, and say to myself, "I hope I am truly awake! Indeed, I am deeply grateful that I was not left to sleep on!" No, I want to escape from threatened death, and so I hasten to the door or to the window, so that I may get out and may not perish where I am. It would be a questionable blessing to be aroused and yet not to escape from the danger.

Remember, **awakening is not salvation**. A man may know that he is lost, and yet he may never be saved. He may be made thoughtful, and yet he may die in his sins. If you find out that you are a bankrupt, the consideration of your debts will not pay them. A man may examine his wounds all year round, and they will be none the nearer being healed because he feels their sting and notes their number. It is one trick of the devil to tempt a man to be satisfied with a sense of sin, and another trick of the same deceiver to insinuate that the sinner may not be content to trust Christ, unless he can bring a certain measure of despair to add to the Savior's finished work.

Our awakenings are not to help the Savior, but to help us to the Savior. To imagine that my feeling of sin is to assist in the removal of the sin is absurd. It is as though I said that water could not cleanse my face unless I had stared longer in the mirror and had counted the smudges on my forehead. A sense of need of salvation by grace is a very healthful sign, but one needs wisdom to use it rightly and not to make an idol of it.

Some seem as if they had fallen in love with their doubts, fears, and distresses. You cannot get them away from their terrors—they seem wedded to them. It is said that the worst trouble with horses when their stables are on fire is that you cannot get them to come out of their stalls. If they would only follow your lead, they might escape the flames. But they seem to be paralyzed with fear. **The fear of the fire prevents their escaping the fire**. Reader, will your very fear of the wrath to come prevent your escaping from it? We hope not.

One who had been long in prison was not willing to come out. The door was open, but he pleaded even with tears to be allowed to stay where he had been for so long. Fond of prison? Wedded to the iron bolts and the prison fare? Surely the prisoner must have been a little touched in the head!

Are you willing to remain an awakened one and nothing more? Are you not eager to be at once forgiven? If you would tarry in anguish and dread, surely you, too, must be a little out of your mind! If peace is to be had, have it at once! Why tarry in the darkness of the pit, where your feet sink in the miry clay? There is light to be had—marvelous and heavenly light.

Why lie in the gloom and die in anguish? **You do not know how near salvation is to you**. If you did, you would surely stretch out your hand and take it, for there it is.

Do not believe that great feelings of despair would better fit you for mercy. When the pilgrim, on his way to the Wicket Gate, tumbled into the Slough of Despond, do you think that, when the foul mire of that bog stuck to his garments, it was a recommendation for him to gain him easier admission at the head of the way? It is not so. The pilgrim did not think so by any means; neither may you. **It is not what you feel that will save you, but what Jesus felt**. Even if there were some healing value in feelings, they would have to be good ones. The feeling which makes us doubt the power of Christ to save, and prevents our finding salvation in Him, is by no means a good one, but a cruel vilification of the love of Jesus.

A friend has come to see us, having traveled through crowded London by rail, tram, or omnibus. All of a sudden, he turns pale. We ask him what is the matter, and he answers, "I have lost my wallet, and it contained all the money I have in the world." He goes over the amount to a penny, and describes the checks, bills, notes, and coins. We tell him that it must be a great consolation to him to know so accurately the extent of his loss. He does not seem to see the worth of our consolation. We assure

15

him that he ought to be grateful that he has so clear a sense of his loss, for many persons might have lost their wallets and have been quite unable to compute their losses. Our friend is not, however, cheered in the least. "No," says he, "to know my loss does not help me to recover it. Tell me where I can find my property, and you will have done me real service. But merely to know my loss is no comfort whatever."

Just so, to believe that you have sinned and that your soul is forfeited to the justice of God is a very proper thing, but it will not save. **Salvation is not by our knowing our own ruin, but by fully grasping the deliverance provided in Christ Jesus**.

A person who refuses to look to the Lord Jesus, but persists in dwelling upon his sin and ruin, reminds us of a boy who dropped a shilling down an open grating of a London sewer and lingered there for hours, finding comfort in saying, "It rolled in right there, just between those two iron bars! I saw it go right down." Poor soul! Long might he remember the details of his loss before he would in this way get back a single penny into his pocket, with which to buy himself a piece of bread.

Now that you see the meaning of the parable, profit by it.

Chapter 2

Jesus Only

We cannot too often or too plainly tell the seeking soul that his only hope for salvation lies in the Lord Jesus Christ. It lies in Him completely, only, and alone. To save both from the guilt and the power of sin, only Jesus is all-sufficient. His name is called Jesus, because *"He shall save His people from their sins"* (Matthew 1:21). *"The Son of man hath power on earth to forgive sins"* (Mark 2:10). He is exalted on high *"to give repentance...and forgiveness of sins"* (Acts 5:31).

It pleased God from of old to devise a method of salvation which was all contained in His only-begotten Son. For the working out of this salvation, the Lord Jesus became man, and *"being found in fashion as a man, he humbled himself and became obedient unto death, even the death of the cross"* (Philippians 2:8). If another way of deliverance had been possible, the cup of bitterness would have passed from Him. It stands to reason that the darling of heaven would not have died to save us if we could have been rescued at less expense. Infinite grace provided the great sacrifice. Infinite love submitted to death for our sakes.

How can we dream that there can be any other way than the way which God has provided at such cost, and set forth in Holy Scripture so simply and so pressingly? Surely it is true that *"Neither is there salvation in any other: for there is none other name under heaven given among men, whereby we must be saved"* (Acts 4:12).

To suppose that the Lord Jesus has only half saved men, and that there is needed some work or feeling of their own to finish His work, is wicked. What is there of ours that could be added to His blood and righteousness? *"All our righteousness are as filthy rags"* (Isaiah 64:6). Can these be patched on to the costly fabric of His divine righteousness? Rags and fine white linen! Our dross with His pure gold! It is an insult to the Savior to dream of such a thing. We have sinned enough, without adding this to all our other offenses.

Even if we had any righteousness in which we could boast, if our fig leaves were broader than usual and not so utterly fading, it would be wisdom to put them away and accept that righteousness which must be far more pleasing to God than anything of our own. The Lord must see more that is acceptable in His Son than in the best of us. The best of us? The words seem satirical, though they were not so intended. What is there about any of us that is best? *"There is none that doeth good; no, not one"* (Romans 3:12).

I, who write these lines, most freely confess that I have not a thread of goodness of my own. I could not make up so much as a rag or a piece of a rag. I am utterly destitute. But if I had the fairest suit of good works that pride could imagine, I would tear it up that I might put on nothing but the garments of salvation, which are freely given by the Lord Jesus, out of the heavenly wardrobe of His own merits.

It is most glorifying to our Lord Jesus Christ that we should hope for every good thing from Him alone. This is to treat Him as He deserves to be treated. Just as He is God, and beside Him there is none else, we are bound to look unto Him and be saved.

This is to treat Him as He loves to be treated, for He bids all those *"who labour and are heavy laden"* (Matthew 11:28) to come to Him, and He will give them rest. To imagine that He cannot *"save them to the uttermost"* (Hebrews 7:25) is to limit the Holy One of Israel and put a slur on His power, or else slander the loving heart of the Friend of sinners and cast doubt on His love. In either case, we would commit a cruel and wanton sin against the most tender aspects of His honor—His willingness and ability to save all that come unto God by Him.

The child, in danger of the fire, just clings to the fireman and trusts to him alone. She raises no question about the strength of his limbs to carry her or the zeal of his heart to rescue her. She just clings. The heat is terrible, the smoke is blinding, but she clings, and her deliverer quickly bears her to safety. **In the same childlike confidence, cling to Jesus**, who can and will bear you out of danger from the flames of sin.

The nature of the Lord Jesus should inspire us with the fullest confidence. As He is God, He is almighty to save. As He is man, He is filled with all fullness to bless. As He is God and man in one majestic Person, He connects man in his creatureness with God in His holiness. The ladder is long enough to reach from Jacob prostrate on the earth to Jehovah reigning in heaven. To bring another ladder would be to suppose that He failed to bridge the distance, which would grievously dishonor Him. If to add to His words is to draw a curse upon ourselves, what must it be to pretend to add to Himself? Remember that He Himself is the Way. To suppose that we must, in some manner, add to the divine road is to be arrogant enough to think of adding to Him. Away with such a notion! Loathe it as you would blasphemy, for in essence it is the worst of blasphemy against the Lord of love.

To come to Jesus with a price in our hand would be insufferable pride, even if we had any price that we could bring. What does He need from us? What could we bring if He did need it? Would He sell the priceless blessings of His redemption? That which He wrought out in His heart's blood, would He barter it with us for our tears and vows, or for ceremonial observances, feelings, and works? He is not reduced to making a market of Himself. He will give freely, as befitting His royal love. The person who offers a price to Him knows not with whom he is dealing, nor how grievously he vexes His free Spirit.

Empty-handed sinners may have what they want. All that they can possibly need is in Jesus, and He gives it for the asking. But we must believe that He is all in all, and we must not dare to breathe a word about completing what He has already finished or fitting ourselves for what He gives to us as undeserving sinners.

The reason why we may hope for forgiveness of sin and life eternal, by faith in the Lord Jesus, is that God has so ordained it. He has pledged Himself in the Gospel to save all who truly trust in the Lord Jesus, and He will never run back away from His promise. He is so well pleased with His only-begotten Son that He takes pleasure in all who lay hold of Christ as their one and only hope. The great God Himself has taken hold of him who has taken hold of His Son. He works salvation for all who look for that salvation to the once-slain Redeemer. For the honor of His Son, He will not suffer the man who trusts in Him to be ashamed. *"He that believeth on the Son hath everlasting life"* (John 3:36). The ever-living God has taken that person unto Himself and has given him to be a partaker of His life. If Jesus only is your trust, you need not fear whether you will be effectually saved, both now and in the day of His appearing.

When a man entrusts his confidence, there is **a point of union between him and God, and that union guarantees blessing**. Faith saves us because it makes us cling to Christ. Jesus is one with God and thus brings us into connection with God.

I am told that, years ago, above the Falls of Niagara, a boat was upset, and two men were being carried down by the current. Persons on the shore managed to float a rope out to the men, who both seized the rope. One of them held fast to it and was safely drawn to the bank. But the other, seeing a great log come floating by, unwisely let go of the rope and clung to the great piece of timber, for it was the bigger thing of the two and apparently better to cling to. Alas, the timber, with the man on it, went right over the vast abyss, because there was no union between the wood and the shore. The size of the log was no benefit to him who grasped it. It needed a connection with the shore to produce safety.

So, when a man trusts his works, his prayers, almsgiving, sacraments, or anything of the sort, he will not be saved, because there is no connection between him and God through Christ Jesus. But faith, though it may seem to be a slender cord, is in the hand of the great God on the shore. Infinite power pulls in the connecting line and thus draws the man from destruction. Oh, the blessedness of faith, because it unites us to God by the Savior, whom He has appointed, even Jesus Christ! O reader, is there not common sense in this matter? Think it over, and may there soon be a band of union between you and God, through your faith in Christ Jesus!

Chapter 3

Personal Faith in Jesus

There is a wretched tendency among men to leave Christ Himself out of the Gospel. They might as well leave flour out of bread. Men hear the way of salvation explained, and consent to it as being scriptural, and that in every way it suits their case. But they forget that a plan is of no service unless it is carried out, and that in the matter of salvation their own **personal faith in the Lord Jesus is essential**. A road to York will not take me there; I must travel along it for myself. All the sound doctrine that ever was believed will never save a man unless he puts his trust in the Lord Jesus for himself.

Mr. MacDonald asked the inhabitants of the island of St. Kilda how a man must be saved. An old man replied, "We shall be saved if we repent, and forsake our sins, and turn to God." "Yes," said a middle-aged female, "and with a true heart too." "Aye," appended a third, "and with prayer." Added a fourth, "It must be the prayer of the heart." "And we must be diligent too," said a fifth, "in keeping the commandments." Thus, each, having contributed his mite and feeling that a very decent creed had been spelled out, looked and listened for the preacher's approval. Instead, they had aroused his deepest pity. The preacher had to begin at the beginning and preach Christ to them.

The carnal mind always maps out for itself a way in which self can work and become great, but the Lord's way is quite the reverse. The Lord Jesus puts it very compactly in Mark 16:16: *"He that believeth and is baptized shall be saved."* Believing and being baptized are no matters of merit to be gloried in. They are so simple that boasting is excluded, and free grace bears the palm. This way of salvation is chosen that it might be seen to be of grace alone.

It may be that the reader is unsaved. What is the reason? Do you think that the way of salvation, as laid down in the text we have quoted, is dubious? Do you fear that you would not be saved if you followed it? How can that be, when God has pledged His own Word for its certainty? How can anything fail which God prescribes and concerning which He gives a promise? Do you think it is too easy? Why, then, do you not attend to it? Its ease leaves those without excuse who neglect it. If you would have done some great thing, be not so foolish as to neglect the little thing.

To believe is to trust, or lean upon Christ Jesus—in other words, to give up self-reliance and to rely on the Lord Jesus. To be baptized is to submit to the ordinance which our Lord fulfilled at the Jordan, to which the converted ones submitted at Pentecost, to which the jailer yielded obedience on the very night of his conversion. It is the outward confession which should always go with inward faith. The outward sign does not save; but it sets forth to us our death, burial, and resurrection with Jesus. Like the Lord's Supper, it is not to be neglected.

The great point is to **believe in Jesus and confess your faith**. Do you believe in Jesus? Then, dear friend, dismiss your fears. You will be saved. Are you still an unbeliever? Then remember, there is but one door, and if you will not enter by it, you must perish in your sins. The door is there, but unless you enter by it, what is the use of it to you? It is of necessity that you obey the command of the Gospel. Nothing can save you if you do not hear the voice of Jesus and do His bidding in deed and in truth. Thinking and resolving will not answer the need. You must come down to real business, for only as you actually believe will you truly live unto God.

I heard of a friend who deeply desired to be the means of the conversion of a young man. Someone said to him, "You may go and talk to him, but you will get him no further; for he is exceedingly well acquainted with the plan of salvation." It was eminently so. Therefore, when our friend began to speak with the young man, he received for an answer, "I am much obliged to you, but I do not know that you can tell me much, for I have long known and admired the plan of salvation by the substitutionary sacrifice of Christ." Alas, the man was resting in **the plan**, but he had not believed in **the Person**.

The plan of salvation is most blessed, but it can avail us nothing unless we personally believe in the Lord Jesus Christ Himself. What is the comfort of a plan of a house if you do not enter the house itself? What is the good of a pattern of clothing if you have not a rag to cover you?

Have you never heard of the Arab chief at Cairo, who was very ill and so went to the missionary? The missionary said he could give him a prescription and did so. A week later, he found the Arab none the better. "Did you take my prescription?" he asked. "Yes, I ate every morsel of the paper." The Arab dreamed that he was going to be cured by devouring the physician's writing, which I may call the plan of the medicine. He should have had the prescription made up. Then it might have done him good, if he had taken the draught. It could do him no good to swallow the recipe.

So is it with salvation: it is not the plan of salvation which can save, it is the carrying out of that plan by the Lord Jesus in His death on our behalf and our acceptance of the same. Under Jewish law, a man brought a bullock and laid his hands upon it before it was sacrificed: it was no dream, or theory, or plan. In the animal victim for sacrifice, he found something substantial which he could handle and touch. Even so do we lean upon the real and true work of Jesus, the most substantial thing under heaven. We come to the Lord Jesus by faith and say, "God has provided an atonement here, and I accept it. I believe in the fact accomplished on the cross. I am confident that sin was put away by Christ, and I rest on Him." If you would be saved, you must get beyond the acceptance of plans and doctrines to resting in the divine Person and finished work of the Lord Jesus Christ. Dear reader, will you have Christ now?

Jesus invites all those who labor and are heavy laden to come to Him, and He will give them rest. He does not promise this to their merely dreaming about Him. They must come; and they must come to Him, and not merely to the church, to baptism, or to the orthodox faith, or to anything short of His divine Person. When the brazen serpent was lifted up in the wilderness, the people were not to look to Moses, nor to the tabernacle, nor to the pillar of cloud, but to the brazen serpent itself. Looking was not enough unless they looked at the right object, and the right object was not enough unless they looked. It was not enough for them to know about the serpent of brass; each one needed to look for himself. When a man is ill, he may have a good knowledge of medicine, and yet he may die if he does not actually take the healing draught.

We must receive Jesus, for *"to as many as received Him, to them gave He power to become the sons of God"* (John 1:12). Lay the emphasis on two words: We must receive **Him**, and we must **receive** Him. We must open wide the door and take Christ Jesus in, for *"Christ in you"* is *"the hope of glory"* (Colossians 1:27). Christ must be no myth, no dream, no phantom to us, but a real man and truly God. Our reception of Him must be no forced or feigned acceptance, but the hearty and happy assent and consent of the soul that He shall be the all in all of our salvation. Will we not at once come to Him and make Him our sole trust?

The dove is hunted by the hawk and finds no security from its restless enemy. It has learned that there is shelter for it in the cleft of the rock and hastens there on glad wing. Once wholly sheltered within its refuge, the dove fears no bird of prey. But if it did not hide itself in the rock, it would be seized upon by its adversary. The rock would be of no use to the dove if the dove did not enter its cleft. The whole body must be hidden in the rock. Even if ten thousand other birds had found a fortress there, yet that fact would not save the one dove which is now pursued by the hawk! It must put its whole self into the shelter and bury itself within its refuge, or its life will be forfeited to the destroyer.

What a picture of faith is this! It is entering into Jesus, hiding in His wounds.

"Rock of Ages, cleft for me.
Let me hide myself in Thee."

The dove is out of sight: the rock alone is seen. So does the guilty soul dart into the pierced side of Jesus by faith and is buried in Him out of sight of avenging justice. But there must be this personal application to Jesus for shelter. This is precisely what so many put off from day to day, until it is to be feared that they will *"die in* [their] *sins."* What an awful word is that! It is what our Lord said to the unbelieving Jews. He says the same to us at this hour: *"If ye believe not that I am He, ye shall dies in your sins"* (John 8:24). It makes

31

one's heart quiver to think that even one who reads these lines may yet be of the miserable company who will thus perish. The Lord prevent it of His great grace!

I saw, the other day, a remarkable picture, which I will use as an illustration of the way of salvation by faith in Jesus. An offender had committed a crime for which he must die, but it was in the olden time, when churches were considered to be sanctuaries in which criminals might hide themselves and so escape from death. See the transgressor! He rushes towards the church as the guards pursue him with their drawn swords, thirsting for his blood! They follow him even to the church door. He rushes up the steps. Just as they are about to overtake him and hew him in pieces on the threshold of the church, out comes the Bishop, holding up the cross. He cries, "Back, back! Stain not the precincts of God's house with blood! Stand back!" The fierce soldiers at once respect the emblem and retire, while the poor fugitive hides himself behind the robes of the Bishop.

It is even so with Christ. The guilty sinner flies straight to Jesus. Though Justice pursues him, Christ lifts up His wounded hands and cries to Justice, "Stand back! I shelter this sinner. In the secret place of My tabernacle do I hide him. I will not suffer him to perish, for he puts his trust in Me." Sinner, run to Christ!

But you answer, "I am too vile." The more vile you are, the more will you honor Him by believing that He is able to protect even you. "But I am so great a sinner." Then the more honor will be given to Him if you have faith to trust in Him, great sinner though you are.

If you have a minor ailment, and you tell your physician, "Sir, I am quite confident in your skill to heal," there is no great compliment in your declaration. Anybody can cure an ache or a trifling sickness. But if you are very sick with a complication of diseases which grievously torment you, and you say, "Sir, I seek no better physician. I will ask no other advice but yours. I trust myself joyfully with you," what an honor have you conferred on him, that you can trust your life in his hands while it is in extreme and immediate danger!

Do the same with Christ; put your soul into His care. Do it deliberately and without a doubt. Dare to quit all other hopes. Venture all on Jesus. I say "venture" though there is nothing really venturesome in it, for He is abundantly able to save. Cast yourself simply on Jesus. Let nothing but faith be in your soul towards Jesus. Believe Him and trust in Him, and you will never be made ashamed of your confidence. *"He that believeth on Him shall not be confounded"* (1 Peter 2:6).

Chapter 4

Very Simple Faith

To many, faith seems a hard thing. The truth is, it is only hard because it is easy. Naaman thought it hard that he should have to wash in the Jordan; but if it had been some great thing, he would have done it very cheerfully. People think that salvation must be the result of some act or feeling, very mysterious, and very difficult; but God's thoughts are not our thoughts, neither are His ways our ways (see Isaiah 55:8). In order that the feeblest and the most ignorant may be saved, He has made the way of salvation as easy as the *ABC*'s. There is nothing about it to puzzle anyone, except that as everyone expects to be puzzled by it, many are quite bewildered when they find it to be so exceedingly simple.

The fact is, we do not believe that God means what He is saying. We act as if it could not possibly be true.

I have heard of a Sunday-school teacher who performed an experiment which I do not think I will ever try with children, for it might turn out to be a very expensive one. Indeed, I feel sure that the result in my case would be very different from what I now describe.

This teacher had been trying to illustrate what faith was. As he could not get it into the minds of his boys, he took his watch, and he said, "Now, I will give you this watch, John. Will you have it?" John began wondering what the teacher could mean and did not seize the treasure, but made no answer. The teacher said to the next boy, "Henry, here is the watch. Will you have it?" The boy, with a very proper modesty, replied, "No, thank you, sir." The teacher tried several of the boys with the same result. At last a youngster, who was not so wise or so thoughtful as the others, but more believing, said in the most natural way, "Thank you, sir," and put the watch into his pocket.

Then the other boys woke up to a startling fact. Their companion had received a watch which they had refused. One of the boys quickly asked of the teacher, "Is he to keep it?" "Of course he is," said the teacher, "I offered it to him, and he accepted it. I would not give a thing and take it back: that would be very foolish. I put the watch before you and said that I gave it to you, but none of you would have it." "Oh!" said the boy, "if I had known you meant it, I would have had it." Of course he would. He thought it was a piece of acting, and nothing more. All the other boys were in a dreadful state of mind to think that they had lost the watch. Each one cried, "Teacher, I did not know you meant it, but I thought..." No one took the gift, but every one thought. Each one had his theory, except the boy who believed what he was told and got the watch.

Now I wish that I could always be such a simple child as literally to believe what the Lord says and take what He puts before me. I would like to be able to rest in any circumstances, content that He is not playing with me, and that I cannot be wrong in accepting what He sets before me in the Gospel. Happy would we be if we would trust and raise no questions. But, alas, we will get thinking and doubting.

When the Lord lifts His dear Son before a sinner, that sinner should take Him without hesitation. If you take Him, you have Him, and none can take Him from you. Out with your hand, man, and take Him at once! When inquirers accept the Bible as literally true and see that Jesus is really given to all who trust Him, all the difficulty about understanding the way of salvation vanishes like the morning's frost at the rising of the sun.

Two inquiring ones came to me in my vestry. They had been hearing the Gospel from me for only a short time, but they had been deeply impressed by it. They expressed their regret that they were about to move far away, but they added their gratitude that they had heard me at all. I was cheered by their kind thanks, but felt anxious that a more effectual work should be brought about in them. Therefore, I asked them, "Have you indeed believed in the Lord Jesus Christ? Are you saved?" One of them replied, "I have been trying hard to believe." This statement I have often heard, but I will never let it go by me unchallenged. "No," I said, "that will not do. Did you ever tell your father that you tried to believe him?" After I had dwelt a while upon the matter, they admitted that such language would have been an insult to their father.

I then set the Gospel very plainly before them in as simple language as I could, and begged them to believe Jesus, who is more worthy of faith than the best of fathers. One of them replied, "I cannot realize it: I cannot realize that I am saved." Then I went on to say, "God bears testimony to His Son, that whosoever trusts in His Son is saved. Will you make Him a liar now, or will you believe His Word?" While I thus spoke, one of them started as if astonished. She startled us all as she cried, "O sir, I see it all; I am saved! Bless Jesus. He has shown me the way, and He has saved me! I see it all." The esteemed sister who had brought these young friends to me knelt down with them while, with all our hearts, we blessed and magnified the Lord for a soul brought into light. One of the two sisters, however, could not see the Gospel as the other had, though I feel sure she will do so soon.

Did it not seem strange that, both hearing the same words, one should come into clear light, and the other should remain in the gloom? The change which comes over the heart when the understanding grasps the Gospel is often reflected in the face and shines like the light of heaven. Such newly enlightened souls often exclaim, "It is so plain; why is it I have not seen it before this? I understand all I have read in the Bible now, though I could not make it out before. It has all come in a minute, and now I see what I never understood before."

The fact is, the truth was always plain, but they were looking for signs and wonders, and therefore did not see what was there for them. Old men often look for their spectacles when they are on their foreheads. It is commonly observed that we fail to see that which is straight before us. Christ Jesus is before our faces. We have only to look to Him and live, but we make all manner of bewilderment of it, and so manufacture a maze out of that which is as straight as an arrow.

The little incident about the two sisters reminds me of another. A much-esteemed friend came to me one Sunday morning after service to shake hands with me. She said, "I was fifty years old on the same day as yourself. I am like you in that one thing, sir, but I am the very reverse of you in better things." I remarked, "Then you must be a very good woman, for in many things I wish I also could be the reverse of what I am." "No, no," she said, "I did not mean anything of that sort. I am not right at all." "What! " I cried, "Are you not a believer in the Lord Jesus?" "Well," she said, with much emotion, "I, I will try to be." I laid hold of her hand and said, "My dear soul, you are not going to tell me that you will try to believe my Lord Jesus! I cannot have such talk from you. It means blank unbelief. What has He done that you should talk of Him in that way? Would you tell me that you would try to believe me? I know you would not treat me so rudely. You think me a true man, and so you believe me at once. Surely you cannot do less with my Lord Jesus."

Then with tears she exclaimed, "Oh, sir, do pray for me!" To this I replied, "I do not feel that I can do anything of the kind. What can I ask the Lord Jesus to do for one who will not trust Him? I see nothing to pray about. If you will believe Him, you shall be saved. If you will not believe Him, I cannot ask Him to invent a new way to gratify your unbelief." Then she said again, "I will try to believe." But I told her solemnly I would have none of her trying, for the message from the Lord did not mention trying, but said, *"Believe in the Lord Jesus Christ, and thou shalt be saved"* (Acts 16:31). I pressed upon her the great truth, that *"He that believeth on the Son hath everlasting life"* (John 3:36); and its terrible reverse: *"He that believeth not is condemned already, because he hath not believed in the name of the only begotten Son of God"* (John 3:18).

I urged her to full faith in the once crucified but now ascended Lord, and the Holy Spirit there and then enabled her to trust. She most tenderly said, "Oh, sir, I have been looking to my feelings, and this has been my mistake! Now I trust my soul with Jesus, and I am saved." She found **immediate peace through believing**. There is no other way.

God has been pleased to make the necessities of life very simple matters. We must eat, and even a blind man can find the way to his mouth. We must drink, and even the tiniest babe knows how to do this without instruction. We have a fountain in the grounds of the Stockwell Orphanage, and when it is running in the hot weather, the boys go to it naturally. We have no class for fountain drill. Many poor boys have come to the Orphanage, but never one who was so ignorant that he did not know how to drink. Now faith is, in spiritual things, what eating and drinking are in temporal things. By the mouth of faith, we take the blessings of grace into our spiritual nature, and they are ours.

I address you who would believe, but think you cannot. Do you not see that, as one can drink and eat without strength and gets strength by eating, so we may **receive Jesus without effort**? And moreover, by accepting Him we receive power for all such further effort as we may be called to put forth?

Faith is so simple a matter that, whenever I try to explain it, I am very fearful lest I should cloud its simplicity. When Thomas Scott had printed his *Notes on the Pilgrim's Progress*, he asked one of his parishioners whether she understood the book. "Oh yes, sir," said she, "I understand Mr. Bunyan well enough, and I am hoping that one day, by grace, I may understand your explanations." Would I not feel mortified if my reader should know what faith is, and then get confused by my explanation? I will, however, make an attempt and pray the Lord makes it clear.

I am told that on a certain highland road there was a disputed right of way. The owner wished to preserve his supremacy, and at the same time he did not wish to inconvenience the public. Thus, he made an arrangement which occasioned the following incident. Seeing a sweet country girl standing at the gate, a tourist went up to her and offered her a shilling to permit him to pass. "No, no," said the child, "I must not take anything from you; but you are to say, 'Please allow me to pass,' and then you may come through and welcome." The permission was to be asked for, but it could be had for the asking.

Just so, eternal life is free. It can be had, yes, it will be at once had, by trusting in the word of Him who cannot lie. Trust Christ. and by that trust you grasp salvation and eternal life. Do not philosophize. Do not sit down and bother your poor brain. Just believe Jesus as you would believe your father. Trust Him as you trust your money with a banker or your health with a doctor.

Faith will not long seem a difficulty to you, nor ought it to be so, for it is simple. Faith is trusting, trusting wholly upon the person, work, merit, and power of the Son of God. Some think this trusting is a romantic business, but indeed it is the simplest thing that can possibly be. To some of us, truths which were once hard to believe are now matters of fact we would find hard to doubt.

If one of our great-grandfathers were to come back from the dead into the present time, what a great deal of trust he would need! He would say tomorrow morning, "Where are the flint and steel? I want a light." We would give him a little box with tiny pieces of wood in it and tell him to strike one of them on the box.

He would have to trust a good deal before he would believe that fire could thus be produced. We would next say to him, "Now that you have a light, turn that tap, and light the gas." He sees nothing. How can light come through an invisible vapor? And yet it does. "Come with us, grandfather. Sit in that chair. Look at that box in front of you. You will see your likeness directly." "No, child," he would say, "it is ridiculous. The sun take my portrait? I cannot believe it." "Yes, and you will ride fifty miles an hour without horses." He would not believe it until we get him into a train. "Dear sir, you will speak to your son in New York, and he will answer you in a few moments." Would we not astonish the old gent? Would he not need all his faith? Yet these things are effortlessly believed by us, because experience has made us familiar with them.

Faith is greatly needed by you who are strangers to spiritual things. You seem lost while we are talking about them. But oh, how simple it is to us who have the new life and have communion with spiritual realities! We have a Father to whom we speak, and He hears us. We have a blessed Savior who hears our hearts' longings and helps us in our struggles against sin. It is all plain to those who understand. May it now be plain to you!

Chapter 5

Fearing to Believe

The fear to believe is an odd product of our unhealthy nature. Yet have I met with it often—so often that I wish I may never see it again. It looks like humility and tries to pass itself off as the very soul of modesty. Yet it is an infamously proud thing. In fact, it is presumption playing the hypocrite. If men were afraid to disbelieve, there would be good sense in the fear. But to be afraid to trust their God is at best an absurdity, and indeed it is a deceitful way of refusing to the Lord the honor that is due to His faithfulness and truth.

How unprofitable is the diligence which busies itself in finding out reasons why faith in our case should not be saving! We have God's word for it that whosoever believes in Jesus shall not perish, but we search for arguments why we should perish if we did believe. If any one gave me an estate, I certainly should not commence raising questions as to the title. What can be the use of inventing reasons why I should not hold my own house, or possess any other piece of property which is enjoyed by me? If the Lord is satisfied to save me through the merits of His dear Son, assuredly I may be satisfied to be so saved. If I take God at His word, the responsibility of fulfilling His promise does not lie with me, but with God, who made the promise.

But you fear that you may not be one of those for whom the promise is intended. Do not be alarmed by that idle suspicion. No soul ever came to Jesus wrongly. No one can come at all unless the Father draw him (see John 6:44). Jesus has said, *"Him that cometh to me I will in no wise cast out"* (John 6:37). No soul ever lays hold on Christ through robbery. He that has Him has Him by right divine; for the Lord's giving of Himself for us, and to us, is so free, that every soul that takes Him has a grace-given right to do so. If you lay hold of Jesus by the hem of His garment, without His leave and behind Him, yet virtue will flow from Him to you as surely as if He had called you out by name and bidden you to trust Him. Dismiss all fear when you trust the Savior. Take Him and welcome. He that believes in Jesus is one of God's elect.

Did you suggest that it would be a very horrible thing if you were to trust in Jesus and yet perish? It would be so. But as you must perish if you do not trust, the risk at the worst is not very great.

> "I can but perish if I go;
> I am resolved to try;
> For if I stay away, I know
> I must forever die."

Suppose you stand in the Slough of Despond forever. What will be the good of that? Surely it would be better to die struggling along the King's highway towards the Celestial City, than sinking deeper and deeper in the mire and filth of dark, distrustful thoughts! You have nothing to lose, for you have lost everything already. Therefore, make a dash for it and dare to believe in the mercy of God to you, even to you.

But one moans, "What if I come to Christ, and He refuses me?" My answer is, "Try Him." Cast yourself on the Lord Jesus, and see if He refuses you. You will be the first against whom He has shut the door of hope. Friend, don't cross that bridge until you come to it! When Jesus casts you out, it will be time enough to despair, but that time will never come. *"This man receiveth sinners"* (Luke 15:2). He has not so much as begun to cast them out.

Have you ever heard of the man who lost his way one night and came to the edge of a precipice, or so he thought, and in his own apprehension fell over the cliff? He clutched at an old tree, and there hung, clinging to his frail support with all his might. He felt persuaded that, if he released his hold, he would be dashed in pieces on some awful rocks that waited for him down below. There he hung, with the sweat on his brow and anguish in every limb. He passed into a desperate state of fever and faintness, and at last his hands could hold up his body no longer. He relaxed his grasp! He dropped from his support! He fell— about a foot or so, and was received upon a soft mossy bank. There he lay, altogether unhurt and perfectly safe, until morning.

Thus, in the darkness of their ignorance, many think that sure destruction awaits them if they confess their sin, quit all hope in self, and resign themselves into the hands of God. They are afraid to quit the hope to which they ignorantly cling. It is an idle fear. Give up your hold upon everything but Christ, and drop. Drop from all trust in your works, or prayers, or feelings. Drop at once! Drop now! Soft and safe will be the bank that receives you. Jesus Christ, in His love, in the efficacy of His precious blood, in His perfect righteousness, will give you immediate rest and peace. Cease from self-confidence. Fall into the arms of Jesus. This is the major part of faith—giving up every other hold and simply falling upon Christ.

There is no reason for fear. Only ignorance causes your dread of that which will be your eternal safety. The death of carnal hope is the life of faith, and the life of faith is life everlasting. Let self die, that Christ may live in you.

But the mischief is that, to the one act of faith in Jesus, we cannot bring men. They will adopt any expedient sooner than quit with self. They fight shy of believing, and fear faith as if it were a monster. O foolish tremblers, who has bewitched you? You fear that which would be the death of all your fear and the beginning of your joy. Why will you perish through perversely preferring other ways to God's own appointed plan of salvation?

Alas! Many, many souls say, "We are bidden to trust in Jesus, but instead of that we will attend the means of grace regularly." Attend public worship by all means, but not as a substitute for faith, or it will become a vain confidence. The command is, "Believe and live." Attend to that, whatever else you do. "Well, I will take to reading good books; perhaps I will get good that way." Read the good books by all means, but that is not the Gospel. The Gospel is, *"Believe in the Lord Jesus Christ, and thou shalt be saved"* (Acts 16:31).

Suppose a physician has a patient under his care, and he says to him, "You are to take a bath in the morning; it will be of very great service to your disease." But the man takes a cup of tea in the morning instead of the bath, and he thinks, "That will do as well, I have no doubt." What does his physician say when he inquires, "Did you follow my rule?" and hears, "No, I did not"? "Then you do not expect, of course, that there will be any good result from my visits, since you take no notice of my directions."

So we, practically, say to Jesus Christ, when we are under searching of soul, "Lord, You bade me to trust You, but I would sooner do something else! Lord, I want to have horrible convictions. I want to be shaken over hell's mouth. I want to be alarmed and distressed!" Yes, you want anything but what Christ prescribes for you, which is that you should **simply trust Him**. Whether you feel or do not feel, cast yourself on Him, that He may save you, and He alone. "But you do not mean to say that you speak against praying, and reading good books, and so on?" Not one single word do I speak against any of those things, any more than, if I were the physician I quoted, I should speak against the man's drinking a cup of tea. Let him drink his tea, but not if he drinks it instead of taking the bath which is prescribed for him. So let the man pray, the more the better. Let the man search the Scriptures. But, remember that **if these simple things are put in the place of faith in Christ, the soul will be ruined**.

Beware lest it be said of any of you by our Lord, "[Ye] *search the Scriptures, for in them ye think ye have eternal life...but ye will not come unto Me that ye might have life*" (John 5:39-40).

Come by faith to Jesus, for without Him you perish forever. Did you ever notice how a fir tree will get a hold among rocks which seem to afford it no soil? It sends a rootlet into any little crack which opens. It clutches even the bare rock as with a huge bird's claw. It holds fast and binds itself to earth with a hundred anchor points. We have often seen trees thus firmly rooted on detached masses of bare rock.

Now, dear heart, let this be a picture of yourself. Grip the Rock of Ages. With the rootlet of Little-faith hold to Him. Let that tiny feeler grow. Meanwhile, send out another to take a new grasp of the same Rock. Lay hold of Jesus and keep hold of Jesus. Grow up into Him. Twist the roots of your nature, the fibers of your heart, about Him. He is as free to you as the rocks are to the fir tree. Be as firmly lashed to Him as the pine is to the mountain's side.

Chapter 6

Difficulty in the Way of Believing

It may be that the reader feels a difficulty in believing. Let him consider that we cannot believe by an immediate act. The state of mind which we describe as believing is a result, following upon certain former states of mind. We come to faith by degrees. **There may be such a thing as faith at first sight, but usually we reach faith by stages**. We become interested, we consider, we hear evidence, we are convinced, and so we are led to believe.

If, then, I wish to believe, but for some reason or other, find that I cannot attain faith, what should I do? Should I stand like a cow staring at a new gate, or, like an intelligent being, should I use the proper means? If I wish to believe anything, what will I do? I will answer according to the rules of common sense.

If I were told that the Sultan of Zanzibar was a good man, and it happened to be a matter of interest to me, I do not suppose I would feel any difficulty in believing it. But if for some reason I had a doubt about it, and yet wished to believe the news, how should I act? Would I not hunt all the information within my reach about his Majesty, and try, by study of the newspapers and other documents, to arrive at the truth? Better still, if he happened to be in this country and would see me, and if I could also converse with members of his court and citizens of his country, I would be greatly helped to arrive at a decision by using these sources of information.

Evidence weighed and knowledge obtained lead to faith. It is true that faith in Jesus is the gift of God, but He usually bestows it in accordance with the laws of mind. Hence, we are told that *"faith cometh by hearing, and hearing by the Word of God"* (Romans 10:17). If you want to believe in Jesus, hear about Him, read about Him, think about Him, know about Him, and so you will find faith springing up in your heart, like the wheat which comes up through the moisture and the heat operating upon the seed which has been sown.

If I wished to have faith in a certain physician, I would ask for testimonials of his cures, I would wish to see the diplomas which certified to his professional knowledge, and I would also like to hear what he has to say upon certain complicated cases. In fact, I would take means to know, in order that I might believe.

Be much in hearing concerning Jesus. Souls by hundreds come to faith in Jesus under a ministry which sets Him forth clearly and constantly. Few remain unbelieving under a preacher whose great subject is Christ crucified. Hear no minister of any other sort. There are such. I have heard of one who found in his pulpit Bible a paper bearing this text, *"Sir, we would see Jesus"* (John 12:21). Go to the place of worship to see Jesus. If you do not even hear the mention of His name, take yourself to another place where He is more thought of, and is therefore more likely to be present.

Spend time reading about the Lord Jesus. The books of Scripture are the lilies among which He feeds. **The Bible is the window through which we may look and see our Lord**. Read over the story of His sufferings and death with devout attention. Before long, the Lord will cause faith secretly to enter your soul. The cross of Christ not only rewards faith, but begets faith. Many a believer can say:

> "When I view Thee, wounded, grieving,
>   Breathless, on the cursed tree,
>   Soon I feel my heart believing
>   Thou has suffered thus for me."

If hearing and reading do not suffice, then deliberately set your mind to work to overhaul the matter, and have it out. **Either believe, or know the reason why you do not believe**. See the matter through to the utmost of your ability, and pray that God would help you to make a thorough investigation and come to an honest decision one way or the other. Consider who Jesus was, and whether the constitution of His Person does not entitle Him to confidence. Consider what He did, and whether this also must not be good grounds for trust. Consider Him as dying, rising from the dead, ascending, and ever living to intercede for transgressors. See whether this does not entitle Him to be relied on by you. Then cry to Him, and see if He does not hear you.

When Usher wished to know whether Rutherford was indeed as holy a man as he was said to be, he went to his house as a beggar, gained lodging, and heard the man of God pouring out his heart before the Lord in the night. **If you would know Jesus, get as near to Him as you can by studying His character and appealing to His love**.

At one time I might have needed evidence to make me believe in the Lord Jesus, but now I know Him so well by proving Him that I would need a very great deal of evidence to make me doubt Him. It is now more natural for me to trust than to disbelieve. This is the new nature triumphing. It was not so at the first. The novelty of faith is, in the beginning, a source of weakness, but **act after act of trusting turns faith into a habit**. Experience brings to faith strong confirmation.

I am not perplexed with doubt, because the truth which I believe has worked a miracle in me. By its means, I have received and still retain a new life, to which I was once a stranger. This is confirmation of the strongest sort.

I am like the good man and his wife who had kept a lighthouse for years. A visitor, who came to see the lighthouse, looking out from the window over the waste of waters, asked the good woman, "Are you not afraid at night, when the storm is out, and the big waves dash right over the lantern? Do you not fear that the lighthouse, and all that is in it, will be carried away? I am sure I would be afraid to trust myself in a slender tower in the midst of the great billows." The woman remarked that the idea never occurred to her now. She had lived there so long that she felt as safe on the lone rock as she did when on the mainland.

As for her husband, when asked if he did not feel anxious when the wind blew a hurricane, he answered, "Yes, I feel anxious to keep the lamps well trimmed, and the light burning, lest any vessel should be wrecked." As to anxiety about the safety of the lighthouse or his own personal security in it, he had out-lived all that.

Even so it is with the full-grown believer. He can humbly say:

"I know whom I have believed,
And am persuaded that He is able
To keep that which I've committed
Unto Him against that day."

From henceforth let no man trouble me with doubts and questions. I bear in my soul the proofs of the Spirit's truth and power, and I will have none of your artful reasonings. The Gospel to me is truth. I am content to perish if it is not true. I risk my soul's eternal fate upon the truth of the Gospel, and I know that there is no risk in it. My one concern is to keep the lights burning, that I may thereby benefit others. Only let the Lord give me oil enough to feed my lamp, so that I may cast a ray across the dark and treacherous sea of life, and I am well content.

Now, troubled seeker, if it is so that your minister and many others in whom you confide have found perfect peace and rest in the Gospel, why should you not? *"Is the Spirit of the Lord straitened?...Do not* [His] *words do good to them that walk uprightly?"* (Micah 2:7). Will you not also try their saving virtue?

Most true is the Gospel, for God is its Author. Believe it. Most able is the Savior, for He is the Son of God. Trust Him. Most powerful is His precious blood. Look to it for pardon. Most loving is His gracious heart. Run to it at once.

Thus would I urge the reader to seek faith. But if he is unwilling, what more can I do? I have brought the horse to the water, but I cannot make him drink. May this, however, be remembered: **unbelief is willful when evidence is put in a man's way, but he refuses carefully to examine it**. He that does not desire to know and accept the truth has himself to thank if he dies with a lie in his right hand. It is true that *"he that believeth and is baptized shall be saved."* It is equally true that *"he that believeth not shall be damned"* (Mark 16:16).

Chapter 7

A Helpful Survey

To help the seeker to a true faith in Jesus, I would remind him of the work of the Lord Jesus in the room and place and stead of sinners. *"When we were yet without strength, in due time Christ died for the ungodly"* (Romans 5:6). *"Who His own self bare our sins in His own body on the tree"* (1 Peter 2:24). *"The Lord hath laid on Him the iniquity of us all"* (Isaiah 53:6). *"For Christ also hath once suffered for sins, the Just for the unjust, that He might bring us to God"* (1 Peter 3:18).

Upon one declaration of Scripture let the reader fix his eye. *"With His stripes we are healed"* (Isaiah 53:5). God here treats sin as a disease, and He sets before us the costly remedy which He has provided.

I ask you very solemnly to accompany me in your meditations, for a few minutes, while I bring before you the stripes of the Lord Jesus.

The Lord resolved to restore us, and therefore He sent His only begotten Son, "very God of very God," that He might descend into this world to take upon Himself our nature, in order for our redemption. He lived as a man among men. In due time, after thirty years or more of obedience, the time came when He should do us the greatest service of all, namely, stand in our stead and bear *"the chastisement of our peace"* (Isaiah 53:5). He went to Gethsemane, and there, at the first taste of our bitter cup, He sweat great drops of blood. He went to Pilate's hall and Herod's judgment-seat, and there He drank draughts of pain and scorn in our room and place. Last of all, they took Him to the cross and nailed Him there to die—to die in our stead.

The word *"stripes"* is used to set forth His sufferings, both of body and of soul. The whole of Christ was made a sacrifice for us. His whole manhood suffered. As to His body, it shared with His mind in a grief that never can be described. In the beginning of His passion, when He emphatically suffered instead of us, He was in an agony, and from His bodily frame a bloody sweat distilled so copiously as to fall to the ground.

It is a very rare occurrence that a man sweats blood. There have been one or two instances of it, and they have been followed by almost immediate death. But our Savior lived

—lived after an agony which, to anyone else, would have proved fatal. Before He could cleanse His face from this dreadful crimson, they hurried Him to the high priest's hall. In the dead of night they bound Him and led Him away. Anon they took Him to Pilate and to Herod. These scourged Him, and their soldiers spat in His face and buffeted Him, and put on His head a crown of thorns.

Scourging is one of the most awful tortures that can be inflicted by malice. It was formerly the disgrace of the British army that the "cat" was used upon the soldier—a brutal infliction of torture. But to the Roman, cruelty was so natural that he made his common punishments worse than brutal. The Roman scourge is said to have been made of the sinews of oxen, twisted into knots, and into these knots were inserted slivers of bone and hucklebones of sheep. Every time the scourge fell upon the bare back, *the plowers plowed upon my back: they made long their furrows"* (Psalm 129:3). Our Savior was called upon to endure the fierce pain of the Roman scourge, and this not as the finish of His punishment, but as a preface to crucifixion. To this His persecutors added buffeting and plucking out the hair. They spared Him no form of pain.

In all His faintness, through bleeding and fasting, they made Him carry His cross until another was forced, by the forethought of their cruelty, to bear it, lest their victim should die on the road. They stripped Him, threw Him down, and nailed Him to the wood. They pierced His hands and His feet. They lifted up the tree, with Him upon it, and then dashed it down into its place in the ground, so that all His limbs were dislocated, according to the lament of the psalmist, *"I am poured out like water, and all my bones are out of joint"* (Psalm 22:14).

He hung on the cross in the burning sun until the fever dissolved His strength, and He said, *"My heart is like wax; it is melted in the midst of my bowels. My strength is dried up like a potsherd; and my tongue cleaveth to my jaws; and thou hast brought me into the dust of death"* (Psalm 22:14-15). There He hung, a spectacle to God and men. The weight of His body was first sustained by His feet, until the nails tore through the tender nerves. Then the painful load began to drag upon His hands and rend those sensitive parts of His frame. How small a wound in the hand has brought on lockjaw! How awful must have been the torment caused by that dragging iron tearing through the delicate parts of the hands and feet!

Now were all manner of bodily pains centered in His tortured frame. All the while His enemies stood around, pointing at Him in scorn, thrusting out their tongues in mockery, jesting at His prayers, and gloating over His sufferings. He cried, *"I thirst"* (John 19:28), and then they gave Him vinegar mingled with gall. After a while He said, *"It is finished"* (John 19:30). He had endured the utmost of appointed grief and had made full vindication to divine justice. Then, and not until then, He gave up the ghost.

Holy men of old have enlarged most lovingly upon the bodily sufferings of our Lord, and I have no hesitation in doing the same, trusting that trembling sinners may see salvation in these painful *"stripes"* of the Redeemer. To describe the outward sufferings of our Lord is not easy. I acknowledge that I have failed.

Christ's soul-sufferings, which were the soul of His sufferings, who can even conceive, much less express, what they were? At the very first I told you that He sweat great drops of blood. That was His heart driving out its life-floods to the surface through the terrible depression of spirit which was upon Him. He said, *"My soul is exceeding sorrowful, even unto death"* (Matthew 26:38). The betrayal by Judas and the desertion of the twelve grieved our Lord, but the weight of our sin was the real pressure on His heart. Our guilt was the olive-press which forced from Him the moisture of His life. No language can ever tell His agony in prospect of His passion. How little then can we conceive the passion itself?

When nailed to the cross, He endured what no martyr ever suffered. Martyrs, when they have died, have been so sustained of God that they have rejoiced amid their pain. But our Redeemer was forsaken of His Father until He cried, *"My God, my God, why hast Thou forsaken me?"* (Matthew 27:46). That was the bitterest cry of all, the utmost depth of His unfathomable grief.

Yet it was necessary that He should be deserted, because God must turn His back on sin, and consequently upon Him who was *"made to be sin for us"* (2 Corinthians 5:21). The soul of the great Substitute suffered a horror of misery instead of that horror of hell into which sinners would have been plunged had He not taken their sin upon Himself and been made a curse for them. It is written, *"Cursed is every one that hangeth on a tree"* (Galatians 3:13). But who knows what that curse means?

The remedy for your sins and mine is found in the substitutionary sufferings of the Lord Jesus, and in these only. These *"stripes"* of the Lord Jesus Christ were on our behalf. Do you ask, "Is there anything for us to do, to remove the guilt of sin?" I answer: There is nothing whatever for you to do. By the stripes of Jesus we are healed. All those stripes He has endured, and left not one of them for us to bear.

"But must we not believe on Him?" Yes, certainly. If I say of a certain ointment that it heals, I do not deny that you need a bandage with which to apply it to the wound. Faith is the linen which binds the plaster of Christ's reconciliation to the sore of our sin. The linen does not heal; that is the work of the ointment. So faith does not heal; that is the work of the atonement of Christ.

"But we must repent," cries another. Assuredly we must and shall, for repentance is the first sign of healing; but the stripes of Jesus heal us, and not our repentance. These stripes, when applied to the heart, work repentance in us. We hate sin because it made Jesus suffer.

When you intelligently trust in Jesus as having suffered for you, then you discover the fact that God will never punish you for the same offense for which Jesus died. His justice will not permit Him to see the debt paid, first, by the Surety, and then again by the debtor. Justice cannot twice demand a recompense. If my bleeding Surety has borne my guilt. then I cannot bear it. Accepting Christ Jesus as suffering for me, I have accepted a complete discharge from judicial liability. I have been condemned in Christ, and there is, therefore, now no condemnation to me any more. This is the groundwork of the security of the sinner who believes in Jesus. He lives because Jesus died in his place and stead. He is acceptable before God because Jesus is accepted. The person for whom Jesus is an accepted Substitute must go free. None can touch him. He is clear.

O my hearer, will you have Jesus Christ to be your Substitute? If so, you are free. *"He that believeth on Him is not condemned"* (John 3:18). Thus *"with His stripes we are healed"* (Isaiah 53:5).

Chapter 8

A Real Hindrance

Although it is by no means a difficult thing in itself to believe Him who cannot lie, and to trust in One whom we know to be able to save, yet something may intervene which may render even this a hard thing to my reader. That hindrance may be a secret, and yet it may be none the less real. A door may be closed, not by a great stone which all can see, but by an invisible bolt which shoots into a lock quite out of sight. A man may have good eyes, and yet may not be able to see an object because another substance comes in the way. You could not even see the sun if a handkerchief, or a mere piece of rag, were tied over your face. Oh, the bandages which men persist in binding over their own eyes!

A sweet sin, harbored in the heart, will prevent a soul from laying hold of Christ by faith. The Lord Jesus has come to save us from sin. If we are resolved to go on sinning, Christ and our souls will never agree. If a man takes poison, and a doctor is called in to save his life, he may have a sure antidote ready. But if the patient persists in keeping the poison bottle at his lips and continues to swallow the deadly drops, how can the doctor save him?

Salvation consists largely in parting the sinner from his sin. The very nature of salvation would have to be changed before we could speak of a man's being saved when he is loving sin and willfully living in it. A man cannot be made white, and yet continue black. He cannot be healed, and yet remain sick. Neither can anyone be saved, yet still be a lover of evil.

A drunkard will be saved by believing in Christ—that is to say, he will be saved from being a drunkard. But if he determines still to make himself intoxicated, he is not saved from it, and he has not truly believed in Jesus. A liar can by faith be saved from falsehood, but then he stops lying and is careful to speak the truth. Anyone can see with half an eye that he cannot be saved from being a liar, and yet go on in his old style of deceit and untruthfulness.

A person who is at enmity with another will be saved from that feeling of enmity by believing in the Lord Jesus. But if he vows that he will still cherish the feeling of hate, it is clear that he is not saved from it, and equally clear that he has not believed in the Lord Jesus

70

for salvation. The great matter is to be delivered from the love of sin. This is the sure effect of trust in the Savior. But if this effect is so far from being desired that it is even refused, all talk of trusting in the Savior for salvation is an idle tale.

A man goes to the shipping agency and asks if he can be taken to America. He is assured that a ship is just ready, that he has only to go on board, and he will soon reach New York. "But," says he, "I want to stop at home in England, and mind my shop all the time I am crossing the Atlantic." The agent thinks he is talking to a madman, tells him to go about his business, and not waste his time by playing the fool.

To pretend to trust Christ to save you from sin while you are still determined to continue in it is making a mockery of Christ. I pray my reader not to be guilty of such profanity. Let him not dream that the holy Jesus will be the patron of iniquity.

Consider a tree which has ivy growing all over it, strangling it, sucking out its life, and killing it. Can that tree be saved? The gardener thinks it can be. He is willing to do his best. But before he begins to use his ax and his knife, he is told that he must not cut away the ivy. "Ah, then," he says, "it is impossible. It is the ivy which is killing the tree, and if you want the tree saved, you cannot save the ivy. If you trust me to preserve the tree, you must let me get the deadly climber away from it." Is not that common sense? Certainly it is. You do not trust the tree to the gardener unless you trust him to cut away that which is deadly to it. If the sinner will keep his sin, he must die in it. If he is willing to be rescued from his sin, the Lord Jesus is able to do it and will do it if he commits his case to His care.

What, then, is your darling sin? Is it any gross wrongdoing? Then very shame should make you cease from it. Is it love of the world, or fear of men, or longing for evil gains? Surely, none of these things should reconcile you to living in enmity with God and beneath His frown. Is it a human love which is eating like a canker into the heart? Can any creature rival the Lord Jesus? Is it not idolatry to allow any earthly thing to compare for one instant with the Lord God?

"Well," says one, "for me to give up the particular sin by which I am held captive, would be to my serious injury in business, would ruin my prospects, and lessen my usefulness in many ways." If it is so, you have your case met by the words of the Lord Jesus, who bids you to pluck out your eye, and cut off your hand or foot, and cast it from you, rather than be cast into hell. It is better to enter into life with one eye, with the poorest prospects. than to keep all your hopes and be out of

Christ. Better be a lame believer than a leaping sinner. Better be in the rear rank for life in the army of Christ than lead the van and be a chief officer under the command of Satan. If you win Christ, it will little matter what you lose. No doubt many have had to suffer that which has maimed and lamed them for this life; but if they have entered thereby into eternal life, they have been great gainers.

It comes to this, my friend, as it did with John Bunyan. A voice now speaks to you and says:

"Will you keep your sin and go to hell?
or
Leave your sin and go to heaven?"

The point should be decided before you quit the spot. In the name of God, I ask you, Which shall it be—Christ and salvation, or the favorite sin and damnation? There is no middle course. Waiting or refusing to decide will practically be a sure decision for the evil one. He that stands questioning whether he will be honest or not is already out of the straight walk. He that does not know whether he wishes to be cleansed from sin gives evidence of a foul heart.

If you are anxious to give up every evil way, our Lord will enable you to do so at once. His grace has already changed the direction of your desires. In fact, your heart is renewed. Therefore, rest on Him to strengthen you to battle with temptations as they arise and to fulfill the Lord's commands from day to day. The Lord Jesus is great at making the lame man to leap like a hart, and in enabling those who are sick of the palsy to take up their bed and walk. He will make you able to conquer the evil habit. He will even cast the devil out of you. Yes, if you had seven devils, He could drive them out at once. **There is no limit to His power to cleanse and sanctify**. Now that you are willing to be made whole, the great difficulty is removed. He that has set the will right can arrange all your other powers, and make them move to His praise.

You would not have earnestly desired to quit all sin if He had not secretly inclined you in that direction. If you now trust Him, it will be clear that He has begun a good work in you, and we feel assured that He will carry it on.

Chapter 9

On Raising Questions

In these days, a simple, childlike faith is very rare. The usual thing is to believe nothing and question everything. Doubts are as plentiful as blackberries, and all hands and lips are stained with them. To me it seems very strange that men should hunt up difficulties as to their own salvation. If I were doomed to die, and I had a hint of mercy, I am sure I would not set my wits to work to find out reasons why I should not be pardoned. I would let my enemies to do that. I would be on the lookout in a very different direction. If I were drowning, I would sooner clutch at a straw than push a life preserver away from me.

To reason against one's own life is a sort of constructive suicide of which only a drunken man would be guilty. To argue against your only hope is like a foolish man sitting on a limb and chopping it away so as to let himself fall. Who but an idiot would do that? Yet many appear to be special pleaders for their own ruin. They hunt the Bible through for threatening texts. When they are done with that, they turn to reason, philosophy, and skepticism in order to shut the door in their own faces. Surely this is poor employment for a sensible man.

Many nowadays who cannot quite get away from religious thought are able to stave off the inconvenient pressure of conscience by **quibbling over the great truths of revelation**. Great mysteries are in the Book of God of necessity. How can the infinite God so speak that all His thoughts can be grasped by finite man? But it is the height of folly to discuss these deep things and to leave plain, soul-saving truths in abeyance.

It reminds one of the two philosophers who debated about food and went away empty from the table. Meanwhile, the common countryman in the corner asked no questions, but used his knife and fork with great diligence, and went on his way rejoicing. Thousands are now happy in the Lord through receiving the Gospel like little children; while others, who can always see difficulties or invent them are as far as ever from any comfortable hope of salvation. I know many very decent people who seem to have resolved never to come to Christ until they can understand how the doctrine of election is consistent with the free invitation of the Gospel. I might just as well determine never to eat a morsel of bread until it has been explained to me how it is that God keeps me alive, and yet I must eat to live. The fact is, that we most of us know quite enough already, and the real want with us is not light in the head, but truth in the heart; not help over difficulties, but grace to make us hate sin and seek reconciliation.

Here let me add a warning against **tampering with the Word of God**. No habit can be more ruinous to the soul. It is cool, contemptuous impertinence to sit down and correct your Maker, and it tends to make the heart harder than a millstone. We remember one who used a penknife on his Bible, and it was not long before he had given up all his former beliefs. The spirit of reverence is healthy, but the impertinence of criticizing the inspired Word is destructive to all proper feeling towards God.

If ever a man does feel his need of a Savior after treating Scripture with a proud, critical spirit, he is very apt to find his conscience standing in the way and hindering him from comfort by reminding him of ill-treatment of the sacred Word. It comes hard to him to draw consolation out of passages of the Bible which he has treated cavalierly, or even set aside altogether as unworthy of consideration. In his distress the sacred texts seem to laugh at his calamity. When the time of need comes, the wells which he stopped with stones yield no water for his thirst. Beware, when you despise a Scripture, lest you cast away the only friend that can help you in the hour of agony.

A certain German duke was accustomed to call upon his servant to read a chapter of the Bible to him every morning. When anything did not square with his judgment, he would sternly cry, "Hans, strike that out." At length Hans paused a long time before he began to read. He fumbled over the Book, until his master called out, "Hans, why do you not read?" Then Hans answered, "Sir, there is hardly anything left. It is all struck out!" One day his master's objections had run one way, and another day they had taken another turn. Each time another set of passages had been blotted out, until nothing was left to instruct or comfort him.

Let us not destroy our own mercies by carping criticism. We may yet need those promises which appear needless, and those portions of Holy Scripture which have been most assailed by skeptics may yet prove essential to our very lives. Therefore, let us guard the priceless treasure of the Bible, and determine never to resign a single line of it.

What have we to do with obscure questions while our souls are in peril? The way to escape from sin is plain enough. The wayfaring man, though a fool, will not err therein. God has not mocked us with a salvation which we cannot understand. **Believe and live** is a command which a babe may comprehend and obey.

Doubt no more, but now believe
Question not, but just receive.
Artful doubts and reasonings be
Nailed with Jesus to the tree.

Instead of raising trivial objections to Scripture, the man who is led of the Spirit of God will close in with the Lord Jesus at once. Seeing that thousands of decent, common-sense people—people, too, of the best character—are trusting their all with Jesus, he will do the same and quit further delaying. Then has he begun a life worth living, and he may be done with further fear. He may at once advance to that higher and better way of living which grows out of love for Jesus, the Savior. Why should not the reader do so at once? Oh that he would!

A Newark, New Jersey, butcher received a letter from his old home in Germany, notifying that he had, by the death of a relative, fallen heir to a considerable amount of money. He was cutting up a pig at the time. After reading the letter, he hastily tore off his apron. He did not stop to see the pork made into sausages, but left the shop to make preparations for going home to Germany. Do you blame him, or would you have had him stop in Newark with his block and his cleaver? Here is an example of the operation of faith. The butcher believed what was told him and acted on it at once. Sensible fellow, too!

God has sent His messages to man, telling him the good news of salvation. **When a man believes the good news to be true, he accepts the blessing announced to him and hastens to lay hold of it**. If he truly believes, he will at once take Christ, with all He has to bestow, turn from his present evil ways, and set out for the Heavenly City where the full blessing is to be enjoyed. He cannot be holy too soon, or too early quit the ways of sin. If a man could really see what sin is, he would flee from it as from a deadly serpent, and rejoice to be freed from it by Christ Jesus.

Chapter 10

Without Faith, No Salvation

Some think it hard that there should be nothing for them but ruin if they will not believe in Jesus Christ. But if you will think for a minute, you will see that it is just and reasonable.

I suppose there is no way for a man to keep his strength up except by eating. If you were to say, "I will not eat again. I despise such animalism," you might go to Madeira, or travel in all lands (supposing you lived long enough!), but you would most certainly find that no climate and no exercise would avail to keep you alive if you refused food. Would you then complain, "It is a hard thing that I should die because I do not believe in eating"? It is not an unjust thing that if you are so foolish as not to eat, you must die.

It is precisely so with believing. *"Believe on the Lord Jesus Christ, and thou shalt be saved"* (Acts 16:31). If you will not believe, it is no hard thing that you should be lost. It would be strange indeed if it were not to be the case.

A man who is thirsty stands before a fountain. "No," he says, "I will never touch a drop of moisture as long as I live. Cannot I get my thirst quenched in my own way?" We tell him, no. He must drink or die. He says, "I will never drink, but it is a hard thing that I must therefore die. It is a bigoted, cruel thing to tell me so." He is wrong. His thirst is the inevitable result of neglecting a law of nature. You, too, must believe or die. Why refuse to obey the command? Drink, man, drink! Take Christ and live.

There is the way of salvation. To enter you must trust Christ, but there is nothing hard in the fact that you must perish if you will not trust the Savior. Here is a man out at sea. He has a chart which, if well studied, and with the help of the compass, will guide him to his journey's end. The North star gleams out between breaks in the cloud; that, too, will help him. "No," says he, "I will have nothing to do with your stars. I do not believe in the North Pole. I shall not attend to that little thing inside the box. One needle is as good as another needle. I have no faith in your chart, and I will have nothing to do with it. The art of navigation is only a lot of nonsense, thought up by people on purpose to make money, and I will not be gulled by it." The man never reaches port, and he says it is a very hard thing—a very hard thing. I do not think so.

Some of you say, "I am not going to read the Scriptures. I am not going to listen to your talk about Jesus Christ. I do not believe in such things." Then Jesus says, *"He that believeth not shall be damned"* (Mark 16:16). "That's very hard," say you. No, it is not. It is not any harder than the fact that if you reject the compass and the pole-star you will not reach your port. There is no help for it. It just is.

You say you will have nothing to do with Jesus and His blood, and you pooh-pooh all religion. You will find it hard to laugh these matters down when you come to die, when the clammy sweat must be wiped from your brow, and your heart beats against your ribs as if it wanted to leap out and fly away from God. O soul! You will find then, that those Sundays, and those services, and this old Book are something more and better than you thought they were. You will wonder that you were so simple as to neglect any true help to salvation. Above all, what woe it will be to have neglected Christ, that Pole-star which alone can guide the mariner to the haven of rest!

Where do you live? You live, perhaps, on the other side of the river, and you have to cross a bridge before you can get home. You have been so silly as to nurse the notion that you do not believe in bridges, nor in boats, nor in the existence of such a thing as water. You say, "I am not going over any of your bridges, and I will not get into any of your boats. I do not believe that there is a river, or that there is any such stuff as water." You are going home, and soon you come to the old bridge, but you will not cross it. Yonder is a boat, but you are determined that you will not get into it. There is the river, and you resolve that you will not cross it in the usual way. Yet you think it is very hard that you cannot get home. Surely something has destroyed your reasoning powers, for you would not think it so hard if you were in your right senses.

If a man will not do the thing that is necessary to a certain end, how can he expect to gain that end? You have taken poison. The physician brings an antidote and says, "Take it quickly, or you will die. But if you take it quickly, I will guarantee that the poison will be neutralized." But you say, "No, doctor, I do not believe in antidotes. Let everything take its course. Let every tub stand on its own bottom. I will have nothing to do with your remedy. Besides, I do not believe that there is any remedy for the poison I have taken. What is more, I don't care whether there is or not."

Well, sir, you will die. When the coroner's inquest is held on your body, the verdict will be, "Served him right!"

So will it be with you if, having heard the Gospel of Jesus Christ, you say, "I am too much of an advanced man to have anything to do with that old-fashioned notion of substitution. I will not attend to the preacher's talk about sacrifice and blood-shedding." Then, when you perish, the verdict given by your conscience, which will sit at the King's inquest at last, will run thus, **"Suicide: he destroyed his own soul."** So says the old Book: *"O Israel, thou hast destroyed thyself!"* (Hosea 13:9). Reader, I implore you, do not do so.

Chapter 11

To Those Who Have Believed

Friends, if now you have begun to trust the Lord, trust Him totally and completely. Let your faith be the most real and practical thing in your whole life. Don't trust the Lord in mere sentiment about a few great spiritual things, but **trust Him for everything, forever, both for time and eternity, for body and for soul**. See how the Lord hangs the world upon nothing but His own word! It has neither prop nor pillar. That great arch of heaven stands without a buttress or a wooden center. The Lord can and will bear all the strain that faith can ever put upon Him. The greatest troubles are easy for His power, and the darkest mysteries are clear to His wisdom. Trust God up to the hilt. Lean, and lean hard.

Yes, lean all your weight and every other weight upon the mighty God of Jacob.

The future you can safely leave with the Lord, who ever lives and never changes. The past is now in your Savior's hand, and you will never be condemned for it, whatever it may have been, for the Lord has cast your iniquities into the midst of the sea. Believe at this moment in your present privileges. You are saved. If you are a believer in the Lord Jesus, you have passed from death unto life, and **you are saved**.

In the old slave days, a lady brought her black servant on board an English ship, and she laughingly said to the Captain. "I suppose if I and Aunt Chloe were to go to England, she would be free?" "Madam," said the Captain, "she is now free. The moment she came on board a British vessel she was free." When the black woman knew this, she did not leave the ship—not she! It was not the hope of liberty that made her bold, but the fact of liberty.

Just so, you are not now merely hoping for eternal life, but *"He that believeth on the Son hath everlasting life"* (John 3:36). Accept this as a fact revealed in the sacred Word, and begin to rejoice accordingly. Do not reason about it or call it in question. Believe it, and leap for joy.

I want my reader, upon believing in the Lord Jesus, to **believe in eternal salvation**.

Do not be content with the notion that you can receive a new birth which will die out, a heavenly life which will expire, a pardon which will be recalled. The Lord Jesus gives to His sheep eternal life, and do not be at rest until you have it. Now, if it is eternal, how can it die out? Be saved through and through, for eternity. *"Being born again, not of corruptible seed, but of incorruptible, by word of God, which liveth and abideth for ever"* (1 Peter 1:23). Do not be put off with a temporary change, a sort of grace which will only bloom to fade. You are now starting on the railway of grace—take a ticket all the way through.

I have no commission to preach to you a limited salvation. The Gospel I am bidden to set before you is, *"He that believeth and is baptized shall be saved"* (Mark 16:16). He shall be saved from sin, from going back to sin, from turning aside to the broad road. May the Holy Spirit lead you to believe for nothing less than that. "Do you mean," says one, "I am to believe that if I once trust Christ, I will be saved whatever sin I may choose to commit?" I have never said anything of the kind. I have described true salvation as a thorough change of heart of so radical a kind that it will alter your tastes and desires. I say that if you have such a change worked in you by the Holy Spirit, it will be permanent. The Lord's work is not like the cheap work of the present day, which soon goes to pieces. Trust the Lord to keep you, however long you may live, and however much you may be tempted. *"According to your faith. be it unto you"* (Matthew 9:29). Believe in Jesus for everlasting life.

Oh, that you may also **trust the Lord for all the sufferings of this present time**! In the world you will have tribulation. Learn by faith to know that all things work together for good, and then submit yourself to the Lord's will. Look at the sheep when it is being shorn. If it lies quite still, the shears will not hurt it. If it struggles, or even shrinks, it may be pricked. Submit yourselves under the hand of God, and affliction will lose its sharpness. Self-will and repining cause us a hundred times more grief than our afflictions themselves. So believe your Lord as to be certain that His will must be far better than yours, and therefore you not only submit to it, but even rejoice in it.

Trust the Lord Jesus in the matter of sanctification. Certain friends appear to think that the Lord Jesus cannot sanctify them wholly—spirit, soul, and body. Hence they willingly give way to certain sins under the notion that there is no help for it, but that they must pay tribute to the devil as long as they live in that particular form. Do not basely bow your neck in bondage to any sin, but strike hard for liberty. Be it anger, or unbelief, or sloth, or any other form of iniquity, we are able, by divine grace, to drive out the Canaanite. What is more, we must drive him out. No virtue is impossible to him who believes in Jesus, and no sin need have victory over him. Indeed, it is written, *"Sin shall not have dominion over you: for ye are not under the law, but under grace"* (Romans 6:14).

Believe for high degrees of joy in the Lord and likeness to Jesus. Advance to take full possession of these precious things. As you believe, so shall it be unto you. *"All things are possible to him that believeth"* (Mark 9:23). He who is the chief of sinners may yet be not a bit behind the greatest of saints.

Often **realize the joy of heaven**. This is grand faith, and yet it is no more than we ought to have. Within a very short time the man who believes in the Lord Jesus will be with Him where He is. This head will wear a crown. These eyes will see the King in His beauty. These ears will hear His own dear voice. This soul will be in glory. And this poor body will be raised from the dead and joined in incorruption to the perfected soul! Glory, glory, glory! Glory so near, so sure. Let us at once rehearse the music and anticipate the bliss!

But cries one, "We are not there yet." No, but faith fills us with delight in the blessed prospect, and meanwhile it sustains us on the road. Reader, I long that you may be a firm believer in the Lord alone. I want you to get completely upon the Rock and not keep a foot on the sand. In this mortal life, trust God for all things, and trust Him alone. This is the way to live. I know it by experience. God's bare arm is quite enough to lean upon.

I will give you a bit of the experience of an old laboring man I once knew. He feared God above all and was very deeply taught of the Spirit. He was great at hedging and ditching, but greater at simple trust. Here is how he described faith: "It was a bitter winter, and I had no work, and no bread in the house. The children were crying. The snow was deep, and my way was dark. My old master told me I might have a bit of wood when I wanted it, so I thought a bit of fire would warm the poor children. I went out with my chopper to get some fuel. I was standing near a deep ditch full of snow, which had drifted into it many feet deep in fact—I did not know how deep. While aiming a blow at a bit of wood, my billhook slipped out of my hand and went right down into the snow, where I could not hope to find it. Standing there with no food, no fire, and the chopper gone, something seemed to say to me, 'Will Richardson, can you trust God now?' and my very soul said, 'That I can.'"

This is true faith: faith which trusts the Lord when the billhook is gone, faith which believes God when all outward appearances give Him the lie, faith which is happy with God alone when all friends turn their backs upon you. Dear reader, may you and I have this precious faith, this real faith, this God-honoring faith! The Lord's truth deserves it. His love claims it. His faithfulness constrains it. Happy is he who has it! He is the man whom the Lord loves, and the world will be made to know it before all is finished.

After all, the very best faith is an everyday faith—faith which deals with bread and water, coats and stockings, children and cattle, rent and weather. The super-fine confectionery religion which is only available on Sundays, in drawing-room meetings, and Bible readings will never take a soul to heaven until life becomes one long conference, and there are seven Sundays in a week. Faith is doing her very best when for many years she plods on, month by month, trusting the Lord about the sick husband, the failing daughter, the declining business, the unconverted friend, and such things.

Faith also helps us to use the world as not abusing it. It is good at hard work and at daily duty. It is not an angelic thing for skies and stars, but a human grace, at home in kitchens and workshops. It is a sort of maid-of-all-work, and is at home at every kind of labor and in every rank of life. It is a grace for every day, all the year round. **Holy confidence in God is never out of work**. Faith's ware is so valued at the heavenly court that she always has one fine piece of work or another on the wheel or in the furnace.

Men dream that heroes are only to be made on special occasions, once or twice in a century, but in truth the finest heroes are homespun and are more often hidden in obscurity than platformed by public observation. **Trust in the living God is the bullion out of which heroism is coined**. Perseverance in well-doing is one of the fields in which faith grows not flowers, but the wheat of her harvest. Plodding on in a hard world, bringing up a family on a few shillings a week, bearing constant pain with patience, and so forth—these are the feats of valor through which God is glorified by the rank and file of His believing people.

Reader, you and I will be of one mind in this: we will not pine to be great, but we will **be eager to be good**. For this we will rely upon the Lord our God, whose we are, and whom we serve. We will ask to be made holy throughout every day of the week. We will pray to our God as much about our daily business as about our soul's salvation. We will trust Him concerning our farm, our turnips, and our cows, as well as concerning our spiritual privileges and our hope of heaven. The Lord Jehovah is our household God, Jesus is our brother born for adversity, and the Holy Spirit is our

Comforter in every hour of trial. We have not an unapproachable God. He hears, He pities, He helps. Let us trust Him without a break, without a doubt, without a hesitation.

The life of faith is life within God's wicket gate. If we have hitherto stood trembling outside in the wide world of unbelief, may the Holy Spirit enable us now to take the great decisive step and say, once for all, *"Lord, I believe; help Thou mine unbelief!"* (Mark 9:24).